TIPS · IDEAS

BEDROOMS

DORMITORIOS

CHAMBRES

SCHLAFZIMMER

AUTHORS
Fernando de Haro & Omar Fuentes

EDITORIAL DESIGN & PRODUCTION
AM Editores S.A. de C.V.

PROJECT MANAGERS
Edali Nuñez Daniel
Laura Mijares Castellá

COORDINATION
Dulce Ma. Rodríguez Flores
Laura Mar Hernández Morales

COPYWRITER
Roxana Villalobos

ENGLISH TRANSLATION
Louis Loizides

FRENCH TRANSLATION
Architextos: Translation Services and Language Solutions.

GERMAN TRANSLATION
Angloamericano de Cuernavaca
Sabine Klein

EDITORES

PUBLISHERS

100+ TIPS · IDEAS
bedrooms . dormitorios
chambre . shlafzimmer

© 2011, Fernando de Haro & Omar Fuentes

AM Editores S.A. de C.V.

Paseo de Tamarindos 400 B, suite 102, Col. Bosques de las Lomas, C.P. 05120, México, D.F.

Tels. 52(55) 5258 0279, Fax. 52(55) 5258 0556. ame@ameditores.com

www.ameditores.com

ISBN 13: 978-607-437-054-6

Printed in China.

INTRODUCTION
INTRODUCCIÓN
INTRODUCTION
EINLEITUNG

If there's one thing that should stand out in a bedroom it's the specific stamp of the person or people whose room it is. The bedroom's design should also closely reflect the lifestyle of its occupants and, at the same time, be in synch with the surrounding environment.

In fact, it is such a personal space that people often want to really make the most of it. This is why it is so important to choose the furniture and fittings that best suit the occupants' habits.

When it comes to decorating a bedroom, shape and size are crucial but what will really define the setting is the surfaces and tones of the walls, floor and ceiling. The tone of the light in the room is also relevant, given that cold tones in the bedroom are conducive to rest, while warmer tones are cozy. The best bet is a combination of the two, depending on how each part of the bedroom is used.

While a bedroom's style is defined mainly by its furniture, the personal touch comes from the interplay between the textures, designs and colors of bed covers, curtains and rugs.

Si algo debe de prevalecer en una habitación es el gusto y la personalidad de quien o quienes la van a vivir. Asimismo, es esencial que el diseño de la recámara esté lo más relacionado posible con el estilo de vida de sus ocupantes y de acuerdo con el entorno que le rodea.

Se trata de un espacio tan personal, que comúnmente la gente quiere aprovechar el área al máximo. Por ello también es muy importante que en la selección del mobiliario y de los accesorios se considere aquellos que mejor se adapten a los hábitos de cada morador.

En la decoración de las recámaras cuentan mucho las dimensiones y las formas del espacio, pero la base tonal del ambiente la dan los acabados y tonos de muros, pisos y techos. Son además importantes las tonalidades de luz que se elijan, ya que en el caso de la habitación, los tonos de luz fría invitan al relajamiento en tanto que los cálidos resultan acogedores, nada mejor que tener una mezcla de éstos según sea el uso de tal o cual espacio en el dormitorio.

Mientras que el mobiliario es el que provee de estilo a una habitación, para el gran toque son primordiales los juegos de texturas, dibujos y colores de ropa de cama, cortinas y tapetes.

Dans une chambre, si quelque chose doit avoir de l'importance, c'est bien la personnalité des gens qui vont y vivre. Il est également indispensable que le design de cette pièce reflète au mieux le style de vie des occupants et qu'il trouve une place convenable dans le paysage environnant.

Endroit personnel par excellence, on souhaite généralement en profiter au maximum. Aussi est-il nécessaire de bien choisir les meubles et les accessoires décoratifs pour qu'ils soient adaptés aux habitudes des occupants des lieux.

Les dimensions, les formes de la pièce sont d'une importance extrême pour décorer une chambre mais ce sont les finitions et les teintes des murs, du sol et du plafond qui définissent l'atmosphère de cette pièce. Le type d'éclairage est également important car, dans une chambre, les reflets d'une lumière froide incitent à la détente alors qu'une lumière chaude fait ressortir l'aspect douillet de l'endroit. Combiner ces deux types d'éclairage est d'ailleurs ce qu'il y a de mieux à faire si l'on veut diviser l'espace en deux parties distinctes.

Alors que le mobilier définit le style de la chambre, ce sont les tissus de la literie, des rideaux et des tapis ou moquette qui, avec leurs motifs et leurs couleurs, singularisent l'endroit.

Ein Schlafzimmer sollte immer den Geschmack und die Persönlichkeit der Person oder der Personen widerspiegeln, die es benutzen werden.

So ist es absolut notwendig, das Design des Schlafzimmers so weit wie möglich mit dem Lebensstil seiner Benutzer zu verknüpfen und in Einklang mit ihrer übrigen Umgebung zu bringen.

Es handelt sich um einen so persönlichen Bereich, dass Leute ihn normalerweise aufs äusserste nutzen möchten. Darum ist es auch sehr wichtig, dass bei der Auswahl der Möbel und der Ausstattungsgegenstände jene gewählt werden die am Besten den Gewohnheiten eines jeden Bewohners entsprechen.

In der Gestaltung des Schlafzimmers ist die Grösse und die Form des Raumes sehr wichtig, aber der Grundton der Atmosphäre wird durch die Oberflächen und Farbtöne der Wände, des Bodens und der Decke definiert. Auch der Farbton des gewählten Lichts ist von Bedeutung, da im Schlafzimmer ein kaltes Licht zum Entspannen einlädt, während eine warme Beleuchtung eher gemütlich wirkt; nichts ist besser als eine Mischung der Beiden je nach dem Nutzen den die verschiedenen Bereiche des Schlafzimmers haben sollen.

Während die Möbel dem Raum einen bestimmten Stil geben, ist das Spiel mit der Textur, den Mustern und den Farben der Bettwäsche, der Vorhänge und der Teppiche elementar um dem Raum Persönlichkeit zu geben.

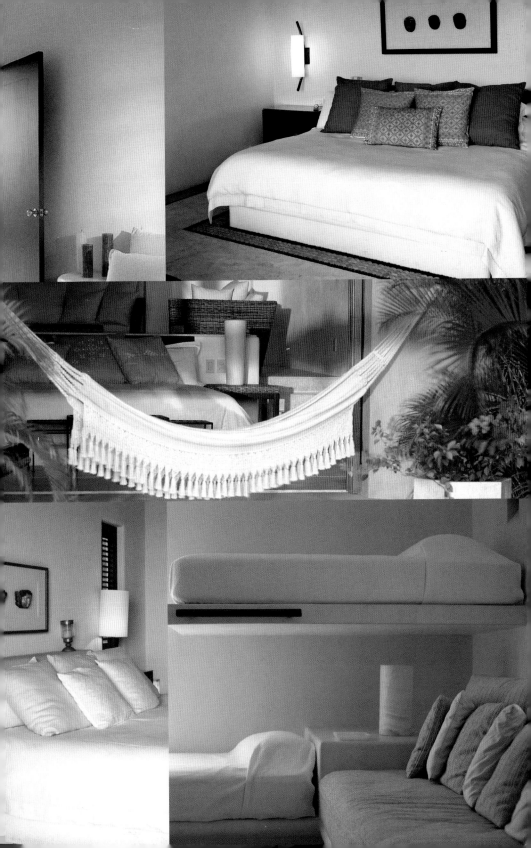

BEACH
PLAYA
PLAGE
STRAND

A carefully selected range of colors and materials is vital for decorating a beach house.

The primary role of bedrooms is to ensure relaxation, but their undertaking becomes all the more poignant in the tropics where they need to ensure tranquility and balance at the same time.

This is why we need to look to blue, green and the range of cold tones in general, as well as whites and raw colors. According to one school of thought, these colors can afford a relaxing quality to a setting. Obviously, bedrooms require brighter tones, even though saturated ones are also a good option.

Furthermore, a favorite in the tropics is furniture made of natural fibers such as liana, rattan or wicker, and it is also commonplace to find architectural or decorative items made from bamboo or reed. Another tropical choice is embedded headboards made with the same materials that were used to build the actual house.

Decorar habitaciones de casas que se localizan en la playa implica la inclusión de una paleta muy regulada, sobre todo de colores y materiales.

Si de por sí las recámaras son consideradas por excelencia lugares para la relajación, su vocación se acrecienta cuando están en el trópico, donde se le exige a estos espacios que mantengan tranquilidad y al mismo tiempo equilibrio.

Por esta razón, hay que voltear la vista hacia el azul, el verde y en general hacia la gama de tonos fríos, así como a los blancos y a los crudos; hay quienes le atribuyen facultades relajantes a las atmósferas que contienen estos colores. Desde luego, para dormitorios conviene inclinarse por los matices claros, aunque también van bien los saturados.

De igual forma, son habituales en los contextos tropicales los muebles de fibras naturales como el bejuco, el rattan o el mimbre, y es común que algunos elementos arquitectónicos o decorativos sean diseñados con bambúes o carrizos. También se usa mucho la construcción de cabeceras empotradas y hechas con los mismos materiales con los que se edificó la propia casa.

Décorer des chambres situées dans des demeures au bord de la mer implique de bien réfléchir aux choix que l'on fait, surtout pour les couleurs et les matériaux.

On considère qu'une chambre est l'endroit par excellence pour se détendre et ce rôle est justement plus important encore sous les tropiques où l'on désire que cet endroit reste une pièce tranquille avec une décoration équilibrée.

C'est pour cette raison que l'on optera souvent pour le bleu, le vert et, en général, pour des teintes froides comme le blanc et les couleurs écrues. Certains considèrent d'ailleurs que ces teintes contribuent à créer des ambiances propices à la relaxation. Il est bien évident que, pour une chambre, on optera en priorité pour des couleurs claires bien que celles qui sont saturées conviennent aussi.

De même, dans des demeures au bord de la mer, les meubles en fibres naturelles comme les lianes, le rotin et l'osier sont habituels tout comme certains éléments architecturaux ou décoratifs en bambou ou en carex. Sont également très employées les têtes de lit encastrées fabriquées avec le même genre de matériaux que pour le reste de la maison.

Schlafzimmer in einem Strandhaus einzurichten bedeutet Farben und Material sorgfältig auszuwählen.

Schlafzimmer werden an sich schon als perfekte Bereiche für die Entspannung betrachtet, diese Bestimmung wird noch gesteigert wenn sie sich in den Tropen befinden, wo von ihnen Ruhe und Balance erwartet wird.

Darum sollte man den Blick auf Blau, Grün und generell auf die kalten Farbtöne richten, sowie auf Weiss- und Naturweisstöne; manche schreiben diesen Farben entspannende Eigenschaften zu. Selbstverständlich sollte man für Schlafzimmer helle Töne wählen, obwohl auch kräftige Farben benutzt werden können.

In tropischen Umgebungen sind auch Möbel aus Naturfasern wie Schlingpflanzen, Rattan oder Korbweide üblich und einige architektonische und dekorative Elemente sind normalerweise aus Bambus oder Schilfgras gefertigt. Auch die Kopfstücke der Betten sind oft eingemauert und aus dem gleichen Material hergestellt wie das Haus selbst.

TIPS - ASTUCES - TIPPS

- *The prevalence of white and raw tones for textiles and walls creates an ambience of freshness.*
- *El predominio de blancos y crudos en textiles y muros inspira un ambiente fresco.*
- *Les blancs et les couleurs écrues, lorsqu'ils dominent pour les tissus et les murs, apportent de la fraîcheur à l'endroit.*
- *Die Vorherrschaft von Weiss und Naturweiss in den Stoffen und an den Wänden erweckt den Eindruck von Frische.*

Framing a
bed within an
architectural
structure is a
good decorative
option, while
some lint and
cotton will bring
out its sensuality.

Enmarcar la
cama usando
una estructura
arquitectónica
resulta muy
decorativo,
usando gasas y
algodones que
lucen sensuales.

Le fait d'entourer
le lit avec
une structure
architecturale est
très esthétique, en
particulier avec
de la gaze et
du coton qui sont
des étoffes très
sensuelles.

Ein Bett mit
einer Struktur zu
umrahmen und
dabei Gaze und
Baumwollstoffe zu
benutzen lässt es
sinnlich aussehen.

TIPS - ASTUCES - TIPPS
- Cream and sand tones are ideal for generating a more subtle ambience.
- Las paletas cromáticas derivadas de los cremas y arenas generan una atmósfera sutíl.
- Les palettes chromatiques dérivées des teintes crème et sable apportent de la subtilité à l'atmosphère.
- Farbpaletten, die auf Creme- und Sandtönen basieren, erzeugen eine subtile Atmosphäre.

The living room's double height is generated by the slope of the architectural structure and, together with the windows looking out into the garden, creates a very attractive area.

La terraza unida a la recámara evoca continuidad y permite aprovechar las vistas como se muestra en este dormitorio.

Une chambre ouverte sur une terrasse contribue à la continuité visuelle et permet de profiter de la vue comme on le constate avec cette chambre.

Eine Terrasse, die mit dem Schlafzimmer verbunden ist, erweckt Kontinuität und erlaubt die Sicht zu nutzen wie in diesem Schlafzimmer zu sehen ist.

Yellow lighting
infuses the
atmosphere with
warmth, while
the colors of the
cushions help
tone it.

Un éclairage
doré réchauffe
l'atmosphère
tandis que la
couleur des
coussins en
atténue l'intensité.

La luz amarilla
hace cálido
el ambiente,
mientras que
los colores en
cojines sirven
para matizarlo.

Gelbes Licht
lässt den Raum
warm erscheinen,
während die
Farben der
Kissen den Effekt
dämpfen.

TIPS - ASTUCES - TIPPS
• The best tool in home design involves opening up views to the surrounding nature.
• Abrir las vistas hacia la naturaleza es el mejor recurso de diseño.
• Prévoir des ouvertures pour apprécier la nature environnante est un outil décoratif insurpassable.
• Die Sicht auf die Natur zu öffnen ist das Beste Werkzeug im Design.

The allure of the space is brought out to its full potential by the diversity of textile fiber and reed textures.

La diversidad de texturas de las fibras textiles y de los carrizos dotan de un maravilloso atractivo al espacio.

La diversité des textures des fibres textiles et du carex esthétise à merveille l'espace.

Die Vielfalt der Textur in den Stoffen und den Gräsern geben dem Bereich einen märchenhaften Reiz.

TIPS - ASTUCES - TIPPS
- A color with presence can transform the headboard into the bedroom's focal point.
- Una cabecera se convierte en el punto focal usando un color con personalidad.
- De couleur originale, la tête de lit devient l'élément décoratif le plus important de la pièce.
- Das Kopfstück des Bettes verwandelt sich in einen wahren Blickfang, wenn eine ausdrucksstarke Farbe verwendet wird.

Sand and
earthen tones
inspired by
the beach
generate a
tranquil mood.

Arenas y tierras
son tonos
inspirados
en la playa
que irradian
tranquilidad.

Inspirées par la
plage, les teintes
sable et terre
apportent de
la tranquillité à
l'espace.

Sand- und
Erdfarben sind
vom Strand
inspirierte Töne,
die Ruhe
ausstrahlen.

TIPS - ASTUCES - TIPPS
- *You can make the most of the available vertical space by placing one bed on top of the other.*
- *Se aprovecha el espacio vertical colocando una cama arriba de la otra.*
- *On profite ici de la verticalité de l'espace en y plaçant des lits superposés.*
- *Der Raum kann vertikal genutzt werden, indem man die Betten übereinander anbringt.*

A highly original decorative effect can be obtained by creating a pattern in natural stone on the bedroom floor to mark the bed's outline.

Marcar el contorno de una cama creando en el piso un dibujo con piedra natural, es un recurso altamente decorativo con un toque de originalidad.

Délimiter l'espace du lit en apposant un motif au sol avec de la pierre naturelle est une décision très esthétique mais aussi originale.

Die Umrisse des Bettes mit einem Muster aus Naturstein im Boden hervorzuheben, ist ein ungemein dekoratives Mittel und verleiht dem Raum ein Hauch Originalität.

TIPS - ASTUCES - TIPPS
- *Purple provides a wonderful contrast with beige to create a fresh and balanced ambience.*
- *El morado contrasta perfectamente con el beige creando un ambiente fresco y equilibrado.*
- *Le contraste parfait entre le violet et le beige apporte à la pièce fraîcheur et équilibre.*
- *Violett steht in einem perfekten Kontrast zu Beige und schafft ein frisches und ausgeglichenes Ambiente.*

The uniform tone of the floor, walls and light creates a visually appealing and homogenous atmosphere.

La unificación del tono del piso, muros y luz produce una atmósfera estética y homogénea.

L'association chromatique des murs, du sol et de l'éclairage homogénéise et esthétise l'endroit.

Die Vereinheitlichung der Farbtöne des Bodens, der Wände und des Lichts schafft eine ästhetische und homogene Atmosphäre.

- The full splendor of textures of natural fibers such as wicker, rattan and liana is brought out by daylight.
- Las texturas de fibras como mimbre, rattan y bejuco se enaltecen con la luz natural.
- Les textures des fibres naturelles comme l'osier, le rotin et les lianes sont mises en valeur par la lumière naturelle.
- Die Textur der Fasern wie Korbweide, Rattan und Lianen werden vom natürlichen Licht hervorgehoben.

A comfy armchair decorated in blue and beige tones marks out a cozy little corner.

Un cómodo sillón decorado en gamas de azules y beiges enmarca un refrescante rincón de ensueño.

Un confortable fauteuil coloré par des bleus et des beiges apporte calme et fraîcheur dans ce coin de la pièce.

Ein bequemes Sofa, in Blau- und Beigetönen dekoriert, gibt den Rahmen für eine erfrischend traumhafte Ecke.

TIPS - ASTUCES - TIPPS
- Stone floors look great and are very practical in coastal settings.
- Los pisos pétreos lucen bien y son funcionales en la costa.
- Les sols de pierre sont à la fois esthétiques et fonctionnels au bord de la mer.
- Steinböden sehen gut aus und sind an der Küste zweckmässig.

Sky blue is
a fresh and
sprightly tone
that can be
combined with
white to produce
a spectacular but
relaxing effect in
the bedroom.

El celeste es un
tono alegre y
fresco, que al
equilibrarse con
blanco produce
un efecto
impactante y
relajante para
este dormitorio.

Equilibré par du
blanc, le bleu ciel,
couleur fraîche et
gaie, transforme
cette chambre en
belle pièce qui
respire la
tranquillité.

Himmelblau ist
ein fröhlicher und
frischer Farbton,
der, kombiniert
mit Weiss als
Ausgleich, eine
eindrucksvolle und
entspannende
Wirkung
auf dieses
Schlafzimmer hat.

TIPS - ASTUCES - TIPPS
- *Two-by-two sequences give rise to a rhythmic pattern in space.*
- *Las repeticiones de dos en dos originan un ritmo espacial.*
- *Multiplier les couples d'objets identiques donne du rythme à l'espace.*
- *Wiederholungen von zwei und zwei geben einem Raum Rhythmus.*

TIPS - ASTUCES - TIPPS
- Generous windows afford a good view of the marine landscape.
- Conviene aprovechar el paisaje marítimo abriendo las vistas con grandes ventanales.
- Il est recommandé de profiter de la vue sur la mer avec de grandes baies vitrées.
- Es bietet sich an die Meereslandschaft zu nutzen und die Sicht mit grossen Fenstern zu öffnen.

The color scheme chosen for the bed can also be used for walls, works of art and any items in need of emphasis.

La mezcla cromática seleccionada para la cama, se puede repetir en muros, arte y piezas de acento.

L'association chromatique choisie pour ce lit peut être reproduite sur les murs et par des objets décoratifs.

Die Farbmischung, die für das Bett gewählt wurde, kann man bei den Wänden, Kunstwerken und Dekorationsstücken aufgreifen.

CITY

CIUDAD

VILLE

STADT

A good starting point for decorating a bedroom in a city house is to look at comfort, especially because this is precisely where people rest from their day-to-day activities. In order to guarantee comfort, it is essential for the bedroom to boast ergonomic furniture, soundproofing and air conditioning.

The need for sensorial quality and coziness in the bedroom is often foremost among the requirements of city dwellers. It is therefore a good idea to make sure that the bedding is delicate in texture, the upholstery is soft to the touch, wood is included in the floor, furniture or walls, and that furniture surfaces are smooth and polished. Rugs can perform a key role in city bedrooms.

As far as lighting is concerned, overhead light is ideal during daytime, while nighttime requires more general lighting along with a few points of indirect light and reading lamps.

Color schemes for walls, floors and ceilings are usually based on creams, beiges and whites, while color combinations and touches will depend more on personal preference.

El punto de partida al decorar un dormitorio de una casa que se inserta en la ciudad es la comodidad. Ante todo, porque la gente utiliza la habitación para descansar de sus ocupaciones cotidianas. Para que exista confort es elemental incluir muebles ergonómicos, aislar del ruido y acondicionar el clima.

También la calidad sensorial y el deseo de hacer de la recámara un sitio acogedor son deseos usuales de la gente que vive en las urbes. Por eso hay que considerar en el imaginario de su decoración que la textura de la ropa de cama sea delicada, que las tapicerías sean suaves al tacto, que esté presente la madera ya sea en pisos, muebles o muros, que las superficies del mobiliario sean lisas y pulidas. Los tapetes tienen un rol interesante en estas habitaciones.

En cuanto a la iluminación, por el día son idóneas las entradas de luz cenital, en tanto que por la noche es necesaria una luz general y algunos puntos de luz indirecta, así como lámparas para lectura.

Las paletas cromáticas para el envolvente rondan entre los cremas, beiges y blancos, y los toques y combinaciones de color varían según las predilecciones de cada persona.

La décoration d'une chambre dans une maison en ville doit être basée sur le confort. C'est en effet primordial parce les occupants des lieux souhaitent d'abord pouvoir s'y reposer et oublier leurs soucis quotidiens. Pour y parvenir, il est nécessaire d'insonoriser l'endroit, de penser à la climatisation et de le doter de meubles ergonomiques.

La qualité sensorielle voulue et le fait de vouloir faire de la chambre un endroit accueillant sont également ce que les occupants des lieux souhaitent généralement en ville. Avant de décorer cette pièce, il est nécessaire de prévoir une texture délicate pour la literie, des tissus doux au toucher, du bois par exemple pour le sol, les meubles ou les murs et des surfaces lisses et polies pour le mobilier. Les tapis peuvent aussi jouer un rôle intéressant dans ce genre de lieu.

Quant à la lumière, les sources d'éclairages zénithaux sont parfaites de jour alors que de nuit, on préférera un éclairage général avec quelques sources de lumière indirecte comme des lampes pour lire.

Les palettes chromatiques pour entourer la pièce vont des beiges aux blancs en passant par des couleurs crème et celles qui attirent le regard comme les associations plus vives dépendent des goûts de chacun.

Der Ausgangspunkt für die Gestaltung eines Schlafzimmers, das sich in einer Stadt befindet, ist die Behaglichkeit. Vor allem weil die Leute es benutzen um sich von der täglichen Beschäftigung zu erholen. Damit es komfortabel ist, ist es absolut notwendig ergonomisch geformte Möbel zu verwenden, den Lärm zu dämmen und die Temperatur zu regeln.

Aber auch die sinnliche Qualität und das Bestreben aus dem Schlafzimmer einen gemütlichen Ort zu machen, sind normalerweise Wünsche der Stadtbewohner. Deshalb sollte man, wenn man sich die Dekoration des Schlafzimmers vorstellt, bedenken, dass die Bettwäsche erlesen sein sollte, dass die Polsterungen weich sein sollten, dass Holz verwendet werden sollte, sei es für Böden, Möbel oder Wände, dass die Oberflächen der Möbel glatt und glänzend sein sollten. Teppiche spielen in solchen Schlafzimmern eine interessante Rolle.

Was die Beleuchtung betrifft, ist am Tag das Deckenlicht ideal, während in der Nacht eine Deckenlampe und einige punktuelle indirekte Lichter, sowie auch Leselampen notwendig sind.

In der Farbpalette buhlen Creme, Beige und Weisstöne um die Gunst und die Farbtupfer und Kombinationen fallen je nach den Vorlieben einer jeden Person unterschiedlich aus.

TIPS - ASTUCES - TIPPS

- Walnut floors look great for areas people pass through on a regular basis.
- Los pisos de nogal son bellísimos y apropiados para espacios muy transitados.
- Les parquets en noyer sont d'une beauté renversante et conviennent parfaitement pour des pièces très utilisées.
- Böden aus Nussbaumholz sind wunderschön und in Durchgangszonen angebracht.

One option for a stylish bedroom is to use fluffy cushions, upholstery with textures that are soft to the touch and a classic rug with flower patterns.

Grâce à des coussins moelleux, des tissus doux au toucher et un tapis classique avec des motifs floraux, on obtient une chambre foncièrement élégante.

Con cojines mullidos, tapicerias de texturas delicadas al tacto y un tapete clásico estampado en flores, se logra un dormitorio elegante.

Mit leichten Kissen, Bezügen mit feiner Textur und einem klassischen Blumenmusterteppich, schafft man ein elegantes Schlafzimmer.

Pure lined and
simply designed
furniture enhances
the sensation
of tidiness and
spaciousness.

El mobiliario de
líneas puras y
diseño sencillo
refuerza la
sensación de
orden y amplitud.

Le mobilier à
lignes pures
et au design
simple souligne
l'impression
d'ordre qui règne
dans la pièce et
agrandit l'espace.

Möbel mit reinen
Linien und einem
schlichten Design
verstärken das
Gefühl von
Ordnung und
Weite.

TIPS - ASTUCES - TIPPS
- A rug with a wavy design will generate a sensation of motion.
- Usa un tapete con dibujos ondulados, te provocará la sensación de movimiento.
- L'ondulation des motifs du tapis donne l'impression de mouvement dans la pièce.
- Einen Teppich mit Wellenmuster zu verwenden, provoziert den Eindruck von Bewegung.

TIPS · ASTUCES · TIPPS
- Lighting can be used to dramatize certain decorative effects.
- Con iluminación se dramatizan los efectos de las telas tornasoladas.
- L'éclairage peut contribuer à renforcer certains effets décoratifs des tissus.
- Die Beleuchtung kann einzelne Dekorationseffekte herausstellen.

The arrangement
of the lights
and the type of
lighting provided
will highlight
and enrich the
patterns on the
bedspreads,
curtains and walls
in a bedroom.

La disposición de
las lámparas y el
tipo de luz que
emiten, acentúan
y enriquecen los
dibujos de las
telas de colchas,
cortinas y muros
de una recámara.

La disposition
des lampes et le
type d'éclairage
choisi accentuent
et enrichissent les
motifs des tissus
de la couette, des
rideaux et des
murs dans une
chambre.

Die zur Verfügung
stehenden Lampen
und die Art des
Lichts das sie
abstrahlen, betonen
und bereichern die
Muster der Stoffe der
Polster, Vorhänge
und Wände eines
Schlafzimmers.

Sleek bureaus look superb next to beds based on straight lines. A longitudinal closet is a practical proposition and can also make a significant esthetic contribution.

Los buroes estilizados lucen bien junto a camas de líneas rectas. Un clóset longitudinal es práctico y puede ser muy estético.

Les tables de nuit stylisées vont parfaitement avec des lits à lignes droites.
Une armoire tout en longueur est également pratique et peut être très esthétique.

Stilvolle Tischchen sehen gut an den Seiten eines Bettes mit geraden Linien aus. Ein Wandschrank an der Längsseite ist praktisch und kann sehr ästhetisch aussehen.

TIPS - ASTUCES - TIPPS
- *Artificial lighting is used to bring out the different architectural details and the texture of the materials.*
- *Un dormitorio que ve a la terraza debe tener puertas plegables o corredizas que liberen la vista.*
- *Une chambre qui donne sur une terrasse doit être dotée de portes coulissantes ou qui se rabattent pour ouvrir la vue.*
- *Die künstliche Beleuchtung hebt die architektonischen Details hervor, sowie auch die Textur der Materialien.*

You can create a work of art along with a sensation of spaciousness by cleverly using a set of mirrors.

Con un grupo de espejos es posible crear una pieza artística y obtener sensación de amplitud.

Avec plusieurs miroirs, il est possible à la fois de créer une œuvre d'art et d'agrandir la pièce.

Mit ein paar Spiegeln kann man ein Kunstwerk schaffen und das Gefühl von Weite verstärken.

TIPS - ASTUCES - TIPPS
• Using a headboard as bookshelves is a highly practical and visually appealing alternative.
• Usar como cabecera un librero es un recurso práctico y vistoso.
• Une bibliothèque que l'on utilise comme tête de lit est pratique et attire les regards.
• Als Kopfstück ein Bücherregal zu verwenden ist eine praktische und ansehnliche Lösung.

TIPS - ASTUCES - TIPPS
- The translucent qualities of onyx can be successfully harnessed for decorative purposes.
- La traslucidez del ónix se puede aprovechar en detalles decorativos.
- On peut profiter de l'onyx translucide en l'utilisant pour des détails décoratifs.
- Die Transparenz von Onyx kann man für dekorative Details nutzen.

Lilac, mauve and plum are colors that inspire distinction and make for a relaxed ambience.

Lila, malva y ciruela conforman una paleta que inspira distinción y hace sentir un ambiente relajado.

L'association du lilas, du mauve et de la couleur prune transforme la pièce en endroit raffiné et calme.

Die Farben Lila, Malve und Pflaume formen eine Farbpalette, die vornehm wirkt und gleichzeitig eine entspannte Stimmung fühlen lässt.

70

A daring presence
can be brought
into the bedroom
by echoing the
motifs of the
bedspread's
patterns on the
wall and using a
lively color.

Repetir los motivos
de los estampados
de una colcha
sobre el muro e
introducir un color
enérgico, hace
que el espacio
luzca atrevido.

Reproduire les
motifs de la
couette sur le
mur et insérer
une couleur vive
dans la pièce
singularisent la
chambre.

Die Motive der
Muster einer
Tagesdecke an
der Wand zu
wiederholen und
eine energievolle
Farbe einzuführen,
lässt einen Raum
gewagt aussehen.

Furniture featuring brown leather and dark wood will contrast dramatically with a few splashes of red in the bedroom.

En esta habitación, los muebles de piel café y madera oscura contrastan dramáticamente con el rojo, al incluir algunas notas en este tono.

Dans cette chambre, les meubles en bois et en cuir marron contrastent vivement avec le rouge placé ici et là, dans la pièce.

In diesem Schlafzimmer stehen die Möbel aus braunem Leder und dunklem Holz in einem dramatischen Kontrast zu dem Rot, das in einigen Details verwendet wurde.

TIPS · ASTUCES · TIPPS
• Long lines on bedspreads, curtains and walls underline the room's spaciousness.
• Las líneas largas en colchas, cortinas y muros reafirman la sensación de amplitud.
• Les rayures épaisses sur les couettes, les rideaux et les murs renforcent la sensation d'amplitude de la pièce.
• Die langen Linien der Tagesdecken, Vorhänge und Wänden bestätigen den Eindruck von Weitläufigkeit.

TIPS - ASTUCES - TIPPS
- *A rug with a curvy pattern will remedy the monotony of a two-tone setting.*
- *Un tapete con dibujos curvos rompe la monotonía de una atmósfera a dos tonos.*
- *Un tapis avec des motifs arrondis rompt la monotonie d'une décoration à deux tons.*
- *Ein Teppich mit runden Mustern bricht die Monotonie einer Umgebung in zwei Farben auf.*

A wooden lattice brings out the visual prowess of a bed's headboard, and this effect can be taken further by adding a couple of bureaus.

Con una celosía de madera se subraya la estética de la cabecera de una cama, solución que se acrecienta al introducir un par de buroes.

Des séparations en bois et percées font ressortir l'esthétique de la tête de lit. Deux tables de nuit accentueront encore l'effet produit.

Mit einem Holzgitter unterstreicht man die Ästhetik des Kopfstückes eines Bettes; eine Lösung, die durch das das Ergänzen von Nachttischen verstärkt wird.

TIPS - ASTUCES - TIPPS
• *White bed linen provides the bedroom with a sensation of cleanliness.*
• *La ropa de cama blanca le da a la habitación sensación de limpieza.*
• *Une literie blanche donne à la chambre un air de propreté.*
• *Weisse Bettwäsche lässt das Schlafzimmer sauber wirken.*

No material affords as much warmth for the bedroom as wood. Desks and furniture for the TV look superb in wood, which never fails to provide visually appealing possibilities.

Le bois est le matériau qui donne le plus de chaleur à une chambre. Les bureaux et autres meubles pour la télé fabriqués dans cette matière sont très élégants et attirent immanquablement le regard.

La madera es el material que mayor calidez le proporciona a un dormitorio. Los escritorios y muebles de TV lucen bien en éste material y siempre es un recurso visualmente atractivo.

Holz ist das Material, das dem Schlafzimmer am meisten Wärme vermitteln kann. Schreibtische und Fernsehmöbel sehen in diesem Material gut aus und es ist immer ein optisch attraktives Gestaltungsmittel.

Decorative details such as amphorae, sculptures, cushions and paintings help provide a bedroom with visual balance.

Detalles decorativos del tipo de jarrones, esculturas, cojines y cuadros, cooperan a equilibrar visualmente una habitación.

Les détails décoratifs comme les grands vases, les sculptures, les coussins et les tableaux contribuent à l'équilibre visuel dans une chambre.

Dekorative Details wie Krüge, Skulpturen, Kissen und Bilder helfen ein Schlafzimmer in ein optisches Gleichgewicht zu bringen.

TIPS - ASTUCES - TIPPS
- Sleek-lined furniture makes the room feel lighter.
- Los muebles de líneas esbeltas hacen percibir ligereza en el espacio.
- Les meubles à lignes fines donnent une sensation de légèreté à l'espace.
- Möbel mit schlanken Linien lassen den Raum leichter wirken.

A small wardrobe is the ideal complement for a bedroom with a high ceiling and the presence of wood.

Un pequeño ropero es el complemento perfecto para un dormitorio que se destaca por su altura espacial y el uso de la madera.

Une petite armoire complète à merveille une chambre qui se distingue par sa hauteur de plafond et le bois utilisé.

Ein kleiner Kleiderschrank ist ein perfekter Bestandteil eines Schlafzimmers, der durch seine räumliche Höhe und die Verwendung von Holz hervorsticht.

TIPS - ASTUCES - TIPPS
- *Cushions and blankets have different textures that are evocative when touched.*
- *Cojines y mantas con diversas texturas son sugestivas al tacto.*
- *Coussins et plaids de textures diverses sont doux au toucher.*
- *Kissen und Decken mit verschiedener Textur fühlen sich verführerisch an.*

TIPS - ASTUCES - TIPPS
- Furniture upholstery is part of the decoration and must blend in well visually with the surroundings.
- Los tapices de los muebles son parte de la decoración, siempre busca armonizar estéticamente con el entorno.
- Les tissus qui recouvrent les meubles font partie de la décoration mais on cherchera toujours à les harmoniser avec l'esthétique générale.
- Die Bezüge de Möbel sind Teil der Dekoration und sollten immer ästhetisch mit dem Umfeld in Harmonie stehen.

In a bedroom with a neutral color scheme limited to white, black and gray, upholstery with good patterns and designs will provide it with a new lease of life.

En una habitación donde la paleta de colores es neutra y limitada al blanco, negro y gris se sugiere jugar con dibujos y estampados en tapicerias para dar elegancia.

Pour une chambre dominée par des teintes neutres comme le blanc, le noir et le gris, on suggérera de jouer sur les motifs des tissus pour apporter de l'élégance.

In einem Schlafzimmer, in dem die Farbpalette neutral ist und auf Weiss, Schwarz und Grau limitiert ist, empfiehlt es sich mit Mustern und Zeichnungen auf den Bezügen zu experimentieren um Eleganz zu vermitteln.

A youthful
ambience can
be achieved in
the bedroom by
including brightly
colored furniture
and fittings.

Incluir en un
dormitorio,
muebles y
accesorios de
de colores vivos,
transmitirá la
impresión de un
ambiente juvenil.

Dans une
chambre, le fait
de choisir des
meubles et des
accessoires de
couleur vive
rajeunira la
pièce.

In einem
Schlafzimmer
Möbel und
Dekorationsstücke
in lebendigen
Farben zu
verwenden
vermittelt eine
jugendliche
Atmosphäre.

TIPS - ASTUCES - TIPPS
• Another option for creating a youthful effect is to put mattresses at floor level, like a Japanese futon.
• Para habitaciones juveniles van bien los colchones a ras de suelo, tipo futones japoneses.
• Les matelas au ras du sol comme les futons japonais conviennent parfaitement dans les chambres d'enfants.
• Für Jugendzimmer eignen sich besonders Matratzen auf Bodenhöhe, wie japanische Futons.

TIPS - ASTUCES - TIPPS
- Scant furniture and uncomplicated designs afford a sensation of visual cleanliness and space.
- Se genera la impresión de limpieza visual y desahogo con pocos muebles y de diseños sencillos.
- Grâce à un nombre limité de meubles et à un design simple, la chambre paraît nette et dégagée.
- Der Eindruck von optischer Sauberkeit und Geräumigkeit wird durch wenige Möbel mit schlichtem Design erzeugt.

In a room featuring contemporary furniture, an old chest will provide a pleasing touch and make a sleek light stand out.

En un ambiente donde predomina el mobiliario contemporáneo, un baúl antiguo da el toque al espacio y hace lucir una esbelta lámpara.

Dans une pièce dominée par un mobilier moderne, un vieux coffre singularise l'espace et met en valeur une lampe fine.

In einem Raum in dem moderne Möbel vorherrschen, gibt eine antike Truhe den besonderen touch und lässt eine schlanke Lampe optisch herausstechen.

COUNTRY

CAMPO

CAMPAGNE

LAND

The countryside is in itself a pleasant setting, which is probably why the word that best describes the atmosphere in a country bedroom is cozy. This is due largely to the extensive use of wood for both the building and the decoration.

Another tool that stands out and is virtually inseparable from the design of bedrooms in these locations revolves around making sure the views of the surrounding natural landscape are unobstructed.

Armchair upholstery needs to be made from thick fibers in neutral tones, while bed clothing should be warm and cushions fluffy.

Other common features of country bedrooms are rugs on the floor, spot and indirect lighting, and a chimney for good measure.

Thick, brick walls and beamed ceilings are no strangers to country bedrooms.

As for color, the most commonly used tones are ochers, beiges and all the different earthen tones, as well as whites.

El contexto campirano es por sí mismo placentero; tal vez por eso, la palabra que mejor define la atmósfera que prevalece en la habitación de una casa de campo es: acogedora. Ello se debe particularmente al uso generoso de la madera tanto en la construcción como en la decoración.

Otro recurso que destaca y es prácticamente indisoluble del diseño de las habitaciones que se hallan en estos sititos es que las vistas permanecen abiertas hacia la naturaleza.

Es también característico que las tapicerías de los sillones sean de fibras gruesas y en tonos neutros, que los tejidos de la ropa de cama sean abrigadores y los cojines mullidos.

Asimismo, son bastante acostumbrados en este tipo de habitaciones los tapetes en pisos, las luces indirectas y puntales, así como la inclusión de chimeneas.

Es común ver un muro de ladrillo, techos con vigas y que los muros sean de buen grosor.

En cuanto al uso del color, los tonos más recurrentes son las escalas de ocres, beiges y todos los matices derivados de las gamas térreas, siendo también utilizados los blancos.

La campagne est un lieu plaisant en tant que tel. C'est peut-être pour cette raison que le mot qui définit au mieux l'atmosphère d'une chambre dans une maison de campagne est celui de chaleureux. Ceci est dû en particulier à l'usage généreux que l'on y fait du bois, aussi bien pour la construction de la maison que pour sa décoration.

Autre caractéristique notable et pratiquement indissociable du design des chambres à la campagne : la vue est toujours dégagée pour donner sur la nature environnante.

Il est également commun que les tissus recouvrant les fauteuils soient de fibres épaisses et de teintes neutres et que les textiles utilisés pour la literie soient chauds avec des coussins moelleux.

Dans ce type particulier de chambres, les murs tapissés sont aussi habituels, tout comme l'éclairage indirect et ponctuel et les cheminées.

Des poutres apparentes et des murs épais et en brique sont de même courants.

Quant aux couleurs, les ocres, les beiges et toutes les teintes terreuses ainsi que les blancs sont les plus utilisés.

Die ländliche Umgebung ist an sich angenehm; vielleicht ist deshalb Gemütlichkeit das Wort, das am Besten die Atmosphäre in einem Landhausschlafzimmer definiert. Das lässt sich zum Teil auf den grosszügigen Gebrauch von Holz zurückführen, sowohl im Bau, als auch in der Dekoration.

Eine andere Ressource, die heraussticht und praktisch unauflöslich mit dem Design von Räumen in solchen Umgebungen verbunden ist, ist die freie Sicht auf die Natur Andere typische Eigenarten sind Sessel mit grobfaserigen Bezügen in neutralen Tönen, warme Bettwäsche und mollige Kissen.

Auch findet man in diesen Schlafzimmern üblicherweise Teppiche auf dem Boden, indirektes Licht, genauso wie einen Kamin.

Gewöhnlich sieht man Ziegelwände, Decken mit Balken und dicke Mauern Was die Farben betrifft, sind die am meisten verwendeten Farben die Skala der Ocker- und Beigetöne, alle von Erdfarben abgeleiteten Töne und auch verschiedene Weisstöne.

Large volumes
and ample spaces
opened up to
nature are where
wooden beams
can create a warm
and comfortable
atmosphere.

Gran volumetría y
amplios espacios
abiertos a la
naturaleza, donde
las vigas de
madera crean una
atmósfera cálida
y confortable.

Une volumétrie
importante associée
à des espaces
amples et ouverts
vers la nature et
à des lattes en
bois transforme
la chambre en
pièce chaude et
confortable.

Grosses Volumen
und weite Räume,
die sich der Natur
öffnen, in dem
die Holzbalken
eine warme
und behagliche
Atmosphäre
schaffen.

TIPS · ASTUCES · TIPPS
• Artificial lighting brings out architectural details such the texture of the different materials used.
• La iluminación artificial consigue resaltar los detalles arquitectónicos así como la textura de los materiales.
• L'éclairage artificiel parvient à faire ressortir les détails architecturaux ainsi que la texture des matériaux.
• Die künstliche Beleuchtung hebt die architektonischen Details hervor sowie auch die Textur der Materialien.

Wooden furniture produces an ambience of informality, which is apt for a teenager's bedroom and combines superbly with brightly colored bed clothing.

Los muebles de madera clara ofrecen la sensación de informalidad que requiere una habitación de adolescentes y van estupendo con ropa de cama en tonos vivos.

Les meubles de bois clair donnent à la pièce un aspect informel qui convient aux chambres d'adolescents et s'associe à merveille avec une literie couleur vive.

Helle Holzmöbel bieten den Eindruck von Zwanglosigkeit, die der Raum eines Jugendlichen erfordert, und passen hervorragend zu Bettwäsche in lebendigen Farben.

TIPS - ASTUCES - TIPPS

• The number of occupants in a bedroom can be increased by fixing the bed to the wall.
• Las camas empotradas a muro permiten ampliar el número de ocupantes en una habitación.
• Les lits accolés contre les murs d'une chambre permettent d'y loger un plus grand nombre de personnes.
• In die Wand eingemauerte Betten erlauben die Anzahl der Benutzer eines Zimmers zu erhöhen.

TIPS - ASTUCES - TIPPS

- Making the most of the natural color of materials is a great design option.
- Un buen recurso de diseño es aprovechar el color natural de los materiales.
- Profiter de la couleur naturelle des matériaux est une astuce recommandée dans la décoration.
- Ein gutes Mittel im Design ist es die natürlichen Farben der Materialien zu nutzen.

Long-stalked red
flowers stand out
in a bedroom
with white walls
and become
the center of
attention.

Las flores rojas
de tallos largos
resaltan en una
recámara con
muros blancos
y se convierten
en punto focal.

Les fleurs rouges
à longue tige
mettent en valeur
une chambre
à murs blancs
et attirent les
regards.

Langstielige
rote Blumen
kommen in einem
Schlafzimmer mit
weissen Wänden
hervorragend
zur Geltung und
werden zu einem
Blickfang.

Using a
partition with
a chessboard
design and
that looks good
from both sides
is a good way
to separate a
bedroom from
the public area.

Para separar un
dormitorio del
área pública es
ideal utilizar un
biombo con un
dibujo de tablero
de ajedrez que
luzca de ambos
lados.

Afin de séparer
au mieux
une chambre
des pièces
communes,
un paravent
avec des motifs
reproduisant un
échiquier des
deux côtés est
idéal.

Um ein
Schlafzimmer von
der Wohnzone
abzugrenzen ist
eine spanische
Wand mit einem
Schachbrettmuster
auf beiden Seiten
ideal.

TIPS - ASTUCES - TIPPS
• Including a space for contemplation is a good idea in a country bedroom.
• En una habitación campestre es una buena idea generar un espacio contemplativo.
• Dans une chambre à la campagne, réserver un espace pour apprécier le paysage est une bonne idée.
• In einem Schlafzimmer auf dem Land ist es eine gute Idee einen besinnlichen Raum zu schaffen.

Rugs, cushions and blankets handwoven in earthen tones combine very well with different types of wood.	Los tapetes, cojines y mantas tejidos artesanalmente con colores térreos son idóneos al mezclarse con maderas.	Les tapis, les coussins et les couettes de fabrication artisanale et de couleurs terreuses sont tout indiqués si on les associe avec du bois.	Die Teppiche, Kissen und handgewebten Decken in Erdfarben sind einfach mit Hölzern zu kombinieren.

TIPS - ASTUCES - TIPPS

- Adjustable armchairs are great for reading, eating or enjoying a spot of sunbathing.
- Las sillas con varias posiciones sirven para leer, comer o asolearse.
- Les sièges à multiples positions sont utiles pour lire, manger ou prendre un bain de soleil.
- Stühle, die sich in verschiedene Positionen verstellen lassen, kann man zum Lesen, Essen oder Sonnenbaden benutzen.

TIPS - ASTUCES - TIPPS

- *A contemporary ambience can also be cozy at the same time.*
- *Un ambiente contemporáneo puede ser al mismo tiempo acogedor.*
- *Une atmosphère moderne peut aussi être très confortable.*
- *Ein modernes Ambiente kann gleichzeitig auch behaglich sein.*

The view from a house standing on the shore of a lake could consist of a boat, so it is a good idea to include large windows.

Una casa que está a los pies del lago, la vista de la habitación podría ser de barco, por lo que conviene incuir vidrios de grandes dimensiones.

Avec une maison au bord d'un lac, comme la vue de la chambre peut donner sur des bateaux, il est recommandé de prévoir des fenêtres de grande taille.

In einem Haus, das direkt am Seeufer gelegen ist, kann das Schlafzimmerfenster eine Sicht wie auf einem Schiff haben, so dass sich grossflächige Fenster anbieten.

One option
for framing the
headboard is to
use decorative
lighting flush
against the wall
turning the bed
into a focal point
by including an
eye-catching
duvet.

Una solución
para enmarcar
la cabecera es
usar iluminación
decorativa a
ras de muro
y hacer de la
cama un punto
focal incluyendo
un edredón
llamativo.

Des sources
lumineuses
décoratives à ras
du mur est une
bonne solution
pour encadrer la
tête de lit et pour
faire de ce dernier
l'élément essentiel
de la décoration
avec, pourquoi
pas, une couette
originale.

Eine Möglichkeit
das Kopfstück des
Bettes zu umrahmen
ist es dekorative
Beleuchtung auf
Wandniveau
anzubringen und
aus dem Bett einen
Blickfang zu machen,
was auch eine
auffällige Bettdecke
einschliesst.

TIPS - ASTUCES - TIPPS
- Raw cotton curtains blend in well with brick walls and look wonderful in a country setting.
- Los cortinajes de algodón crudo armonizan con los muros de ladrillo y lucen únicos en un ambiente de campo.
- Les rideaux en coton naturel vont fort bien avec les murs de briques et ont un aspect inoubliable à la campagne.
- Gardinen aus roher Baumwolle harmonisieren mit den Ziegelsteinwänden und sehen in einem ländlichen Ambiente einmalig aus.

A warm chimney and a couple of comfy armchairs provide the ideal complement for a small table.

Una cálida chimenea y un par de cómodos sillones, son el complemento perfecto de una mesita.

Une cheminée efficace et deux fauteuils confortables sont des compléments parfaits pour une petite table.

Ein warmer Kamin und ein paar bequeme Sessel sind eine perfekte Ergänzung für einen kleinen Tisch.

TIPS - ASTUCES - TIPPS
• The combination of generous cushions and padded headboards means a cozy bedroom.
• La combinación de cojines pachones y cabeceras mullidas reflejan un espacio acogedor.
• Ajouter des coussins bien rembourrés à une tête de lit pratique renforce l'aspect confortable de la chambre.
• Die Kombination von flauschigen Kissen und gepolsterten Kopfstücken reflektieren einen behaglichen Raum.

TIPS - ASTUCES - TIPPS
- *The richness of materials and textures can utterly transform a bedroom.*
- *La riqueza de materiales y texturas se ve espléndida en un dormitorio.*
- *La richesse des matériaux et des textures resplendit dans une chambre.*
- *Der Material- und Texturreichtum sieht in einem Schlafzimmer grossartig aus.*

The exclusive use of bare materials and furniture in wood tones can generate a warm atmosphere.

Una atmósfera cálida se puede lograr al dejar todos los materiales aparentes e incluir los muebles en tonos madera.

En laissant les matériaux dans leur état naturel matériaux dans leur état naturel comme les meubles en bois, on réchauffe l'atmosphère de la chambre.

Man kann eine warme Atmosphäre erreichen indem man alle Materialien in Naturzustand belässt und Möbel in Holztönen verwendet.

The different tones of wood used for furniture, floors, beams and doors can be changed around to create a whole with the bed clothing.

Los distintos tonos de las maderas de muebles, pisos, vigas y puertas se entremezclan formando una unidad con la ropa de cama.

Les différentes teintes du bois des meubles, du sol, des poutres et des portes s'associent pour constituer un tout qui se marie totalement avec la literie.

Die verschiedenen Die Holzfarbtöne der Möbel, Böden, Balken und Türen vermischen sich und formen eine Einheit mit der Bettwäsche.

TIPS - ASTUCES - TIPPS
- *Stools and armchairs with footrests are comfortable for reading.*
- *Los taburetes y sillones con pieceras son cómodos para la lectura.*
- *Les tabourets et autres fauteuils avec poufs permettent de lire confortablement.*
- *Sessel und Sessel mit Fusshockern sind bequem zum Lesen.*

TIPS - ASTUCES - TIPPS
- A leather armchair looks good in a countryside setting and makes a splendid addition to the bedroom.
- Un sillón de piel va bien en el campo y se integra maravillosamente en la habitación.
- Un fauteuil en cuir convient bien dans une maison à la campagne et se fond à merveille dans la chambre.
- Ein Ledersessel passt gut in die ländliche Umgebung und lässt sich wunderbar in den Raum integrieren.

One way
to boost the
countryside's
presence in the
bedroom is to
have a window
looking out on
to a serene
landscape.

Una alternativa
para dar el toque
campirano a
un dormitorio
campestre es
tener una ventana
que llene de
tranquilidad.

Si l'on veut
vraiment profiter
de la campagne,
une façon
d'y parvenir
consistera à
prévoir une
fenêtre donnant
sur un calme
paysage.

Eine Alternative um
dem Schlafzimmer
einen ländlicheren
touch zu geben
ist es ein Fenster
zu haben, das
den Blick auf eine
ruhige Landschaft
freigibt.

There is nothing
better than a
leather armchair
by the fire for
enjoying natural
surroundings. It
also creates an
exquisite contrast
with the green
tones of plants.

Un sillón de piel
para disfrutar del
paisaje natural
junto al fuego
es maravilloso
y contrasta
soberbio junto
al verde de las
plantas.

Un fauteuil en
cuir près du feu
pour apprécier le
paysage naturel
est merveilleux
et contraste
formidablement
avec le vert des
plantes à ses côtés.

Ein Ledersessel
vor dem Feuer ist
wunderbar um
die natürliche
Landschaft zu
geniessen und
steht in herrlichem
Kontrast zu
dem Grün der
Pflanzen.

TIPS · ASTUCES · TIPPS
- The chimney is a great candidate for the task of infusing the bedroom with a touch of distinction.
- La chimenea podría ser el elemento que le aporte distinción al dormitorio.
- La cheminée peut être l'élément essentiel pour esthétiser une chambre.
- Der Kamin kann zur Vornehmheit eines Schlafzimmers beitragen.

TIPS - ASTUCES - TIPPS
- *Lighting highlights the textural richness of the bed clothing.*
- *A través de la iluminación se resaltan las texturas de la ropa de cama.*
- *L'éclairage permet de mettre en valeur les textures de la literie.*
- *Die Beleuchtung lässt die Textur der Bettwäsche hervorstehen.*

Very bright pinks and brick, combined with wood in reddish tones, will bring warmth into the atmosphere of a bedroom with high wooden ceilings.

Gamas muy claras del rosa y del ladrillo, combinadas con madera rojiza, le dan una personalidad cálida al ambiente de un dormitorio con techos altos y en madera.

Des gammes de couleurs qui vont du rose au rouge brique, associées à des bois rouge-brun, personnalisent et réchauffent l'atmosphère d'une chambre haute de plafond et tout en bois.

Sehr helle Rosa- und Ziegeltöne, kombiniert mit rötlichem Holz, geben einem Schlafzimmer mit hoher Holzdecke eine warme Ausstrahlung.

architecture   arquitectónicos   architectoniques   architektonische

coghlan y covadonga hernández garcía,
(bottom) ELÍAS RIZO ARQUITECTOS, elías rizo
82-83 KARAT, karla atristain rodríguez
85 (top) GRUPO LBC, alfonso lópez baz y javier
calleja, (bottom) ARTECK / TORBELI, francisco
guzmán giraud / elena talavera
86 MARQCÓ, mariángel álvarez coghlan
y covadonga hernández garcía
87 (top) ELÍAS RIZO ARQUITECTOS, elías rizo,
(bottom) MARQCÓ, mariangel álvarez coghlan
y covadonga hernández garcía
88-89 GA GRUPO ARQUITECTURA,
daniel álvarez
90-91 GUTIÉRREZ-ALONSO ARQUITECTOS,
ángel alonso chein y eduardo gutiérrez guzmán
93 (top) C-CHIC, olga mussali h. y sara mizrahi,
(bottom) ABAX, fernando de haro, jesús fernández,
omar fuentes y bertha figueroa
94 SERRANO MONJARRAZ ARQUITECTOS,
juan pablo serrano y rafael monjarraz
95 (top) ART ARQUITECTOS, antonio rueda ventosa,
(bottom) ABAX, fernando de haro, jesús fernández,
omar fuentes y bertha figueroa
96-97 DIARQ, gina diez barroso de franklin
100 ECLÉCTICA, mónica hernández sadurní
104 ADI, gina parlange pizarro
106-107 ABAX, fernando de haro, jesús
fernández, omar fuentes y bertha figueroa
108-109 GRUPO ARQUITECTÓNICA,
genaro nieto ituarte
111 ARTECK, francisco guzmán giraud
112-113 GÓMEZ CRESPO ARQUITECTOS,
federico gómez crespo a. y federico gómez
crespo g.
114 ESTUDIO MANOLO MESTRE, manuel
mestre
115 (top) CÉLULA ARQUITECTURA, benjamín

gonzález y jorge covarrubias, (bottom) GRUPO
ARQUITECTÓNICA, genaro nieto ituarte
116 MEMORIA CASTIZA, marco polo hernández
117 ESTUDIO MANOLO MESTRE, manuel mestre
118 MARTÍNEZ&SORDO, luis martín sordo
y juan salvador martínez
119 DE YTURBE ARQUITECTOS, josé de yturbe
sordo y josé de iturbe bernal
120-121 ELÍAS RIZO ARQUITECTOS, elías rizo
122 EL TERCER MURO, ARQUITECTURA
E INTERIORISMO, enrique fuertes bojorges
123 TERRÉS, javier valenzuela gorospe,
fernando valenzuela gorospe y guillermo
valenzuela gorospe
124 COVILHA, maribel gonzález de danel,
mely gonzález de furber, blanca gonzález
de olivarrieta y claudia goudet de gonzález
125 MARQCÓ, mariángel álvarez coghlan
y covadonga hernández garcía
127 (top) DIARQ, gina diez barroso de franklin,
(bottom) FÉLIX BLANCO, félix blanco martínez
128 FÉLIX BLANCO, félix blanco martínez
129 MARQCÓ, mariángel álvarez coghlan
y covadonga hernández garcía
130-131 COVILHA, maribel gonzález, mely
gonzález, blanca gonzález y claudia goudet

photography   fotográficos   photographiques   fotografische

alberto moreno - pgs. 90-91

aldo moreno - pgs. 70-71

alejandro catalá - pgs. 60-61

alfonso de béjar - pgs. 32, 112-113

andrés cortina - pg. 28

cathie ferguson - pgs. 30-31, 35, 38-39

cecilia del olmo - pgs. 20 (top), 45, 48-49

daniel galindo sánchez - pg. 73 (bottom)

eric lira - pg. 93 (top)

fabiola menchelli - pgs. 73 (top), 123

francisco quezada - pgs. 6-7, 76-77, 96-97

fernando cordero - pgs. 62, 63 (bottom)

héctor velasco facio - pgs. 36, 40, 53, 81 (top), 85, 86, 87 (bottom), 107, 108-109, 115 (bottom), 118, 124, 125, 127 (top), 129, 130-131

jaime navarro - pgs. 59 (bottom), 74-75, 104

jorge garcía cantú - pgs. 127 (bottom), 128

jorge taboada - pgs. 3, 59 (top), 66 (top), 68-69

jorge silva - pg. 122

leonardo walter - pgs. 21, 57 (top)

lourdes legorreta - pgs. 115 (top), 119

marcos garcía - pgs. 66 (bottom), 81 (bottom), 87 (top), 120-121

marisol paredes - pgs. 56, 95 (top)

mark callanan - pgs. 11, 33 (top), 42-43

martha lilián tinóco - pgs. 20 (top), 44-45, 48-49

mary carmen villanueva - pg. 111

michael calderwood - pgs. 16, 20 (bottom), 22-23, 25-27, 29, 33 (bottom), 37, 41,106, 114, 115, 117

miguel garcía - pgs. 46-47

paul rivera - pg. 80

paul czitrom - pgs. 4-5, 78-79, 88-89

ricardo janet - pgs. 64-65

rolando white - pg. 116

sandra pereznieto - pg. 94

sean boggs - pgs. 93 (bottom), 95 (bottom)

sebastián saldivar - pg. 100

verónica garcía - pgs. 82-83

víctor benítez - pgs. 57 (bottom), 63 (top)

Editado en Septiembre del 2009. Impreso en
China. El cuidado de edición estuvo a cargo de
AM Editores S.A. de C.V. Edited in September
2009. Printed in China. Published by AM Editores
S.A. de C.V.